Services for Special Days

Services for Special Days

A COLLECTION

Abingdon Press

SERVICES FOR SPECIAL DAYS: A COLLECTION

Copyright © 1987 by Abingdon Press

ISBN 0-687-38096-0

94 95 96 97 98 99 00 01 02 03 04 — 10 9 8 7 6 5 4
MANUFACTURED IN THE UNITED STATES OF AMERICA

Contents

Note to the User

These services have been collected from a variety of sources produced by different church bodies. Minor changes in format and wording have been made, in an effort to make the collection more uniform. Optional responses, including congregational material, are indicated by brackets. Congregational responses are indicated by boldface type.

Wesley Covenant Service

An order of worship for such as would enter into or renew their covenant with God. For use in a Watch Night service, on the first Sunday of the year, or other occasion.

Let the service of worship begin at the time appointed. Let the people kneel or bow in silent prayer upon entering the sanctuary.

The following or some other suitable hymn shall be sung: "Come, Let Us Use the Grace Divine."

After this the minister shall say,

Let us pray.
Almighty God, unto whom all hearts are open, all desires known, and from whom no secrets are hid: Cleanse the thoughts of our hearts by the inspiration of thy Holy Spirit, that we may perfectly love thee, and worthily magnify thy holy name; through Christ our Lord. Amen.

Then all shall say,

Our Father, who art in heaven, hallowed be thy name. Thy kingdom come, thy will be done on earth as it is in heaven. Give us this day our daily bread. And forgive us our trespasses, as we forgive those who trespass against us. And lead us not into temptation, but deliver us from evil. For thine is the kingdom, and the power, and the glory, forever. Amen.

Then shall be read John 15:1-8, the people being seated.

Then the minister shall say,

Dearly beloved, the Christian life, to which we are called, is a life in Christ, redeemed from sin by him, and through him consecrated to God. Upon this life we have entered, having been admitted into that new covenant of which our Lord Jesus Christ is mediator, and which he sealed with his own blood, that it might stand forever.

On one side the covenant is God's promise that he will fulfill in and through us all that he declared in Jesus Christ, who is the author and perfecter of our faith. That his promise still stands we are sure, for we have known his goodness and proved his grace in our lives day by day.

On the other side we stand pledged to live no more unto ourselves, but to him who loved us and gave himself for us and called us to serve him that the purposes of his coming be fulfilled.

From time to time we renew our vows of consecration, especially when we gather at the table of the Lord; but on this day we meet expressly, as generations of our fathers have met, that we may joyfully and solemnly renew the covenant which bound them and binds us to God.

Let us then, remembering the mercies of God and the hope of his calling, examine ourselves by the light of his Spirit, that we may see wherein we have failed or fallen short in faith and practice and, considering all that this covenant means, may give ourselves anew to God.

ADORATION

Then the minister shall say, the people responding,

Let us adore the Father, the God of love who created us;
who every moment preserves and sustains us;
who has loved us with an everlasting love, and given us the light of the knowledge of his glory in the face of Jesus Christ.

We praise thee, O God; we acknowledge thee to be the Lord.

Let us glory in the grace of our Lord Jesus Christ;
who, though he was rich, yet for our sakes became poor;
who went about doing good and preaching the Gospel of the kingdom;
who was tempted in all points like as we are, yet without sin;
who became obedient unto death, even the death of the cross;
who was dead, and liveth for evermore;
who opened the kingdom of heaven to all believers;
who sitteth at the right hand in the glory of the Father.

Thou art the King of glory, O Christ.

Let us rejoice in the fellowship of the Holy Spirit, the Lord and giver of life, by whom we are born into the family of God, and made members of the body of Christ;
whose witness confirms us;
whose wisdom teaches us;
whose power enables us;
who waits to do for us exceeding abundantly above all that we ask or think.

All praise to thee, O Holy Spirit. Amen.

Here shall follow a period of silent prayer.

THANKSGIVING

Then the minister shall say, the people responding,

Let us rise and give thanks to God for his manifold mercies.

Here let the people stand.

O God our Father, the fountain of all goodness, who hast been gracious to us through all the years of our life: We give thee thanks for thy loving-kindness which hath filled our days and brought us to this time and place.

We praise thy holy name, O Lord.

Thou hast given us life and reason, and set us in a world which is full of thy glory. Thou hast comforted us with kindred and friends, and ministered to us through the hands and minds of our fellows.

We praise thy holy name, O Lord.

Thou hast set in our hearts a hunger for thee, and given us thy peace. Thou hast redeemed us and called us to a high calling in Christ Jesus. Thou hast given us a place in the fellowship of thy Spirit and the witness of thy Church.

We praise thy holy name, O Lord.

In darkness thou hast been our light, in adversity and temptation a rock of strength, in our joys the very spirit of joy, in our labors the all-sufficient reward.

We praise thy holy name, O Lord.

Thou hast remembered us when we have forgotten thee, followed us even when we fled from thee, met us with forgiveness when we turned back to thee. For all thy long-suffering and the abundance of thy grace,

We praise thy holy name, O Lord. Amen.

Here shall follow a period of silent prayer, the people seated.

CONFESSION

Then the minister shall say, the people responding,

Let us now examine ourselves before God, humbly confessing our sins and watching our hearts, lest by self-deceit we shut ourselves out from his presence. Let us pray.
O God our Father, who has set forth the way of life for us in thy beloved Son: We confess with shame our slowness to learn of him, our reluctance to follow him.

Thou hast spoken and called, and we have not given heed; thy beauty hath shone forth, and we have been blind; thou hast stretched out thy hands to us through our fellows, and we have passed by. We have taken great benefits with little thanks; we have been unworthy of thy changeless love.

Have mercy upon us and forgive us, O Lord.

Forgive us, we beseech thee, the poverty of our worship, the formality and selfishness of our prayers, our inconstancy and unbelief, our neglect of fellowship and of the means of grace, our hesitating witness for Christ, our false pretenses, and our willful ignorance of thy ways.

Have mercy upon us and forgive us, O Lord.

Forgive us wherein we have wasted our time or misused our gifts. Forgive us wherein we have excused our own wrongdoing or evaded our responsibilities. Forgive us that we have been unwilling to overcome evil with good, that we have drawn back from the cross.

Have mercy upon us and forgive us, O Lord.

Forgive us that so little of thy love hath reached others through us, and that we have borne so lightly wrongs and sufferings that were not our own. Forgive us wherein we have cherished the things that divide us from others, and wherein we have made it hard for them to live with us, and wherein we have been thoughtless in our judgments, hasty in condemnation, grudging in forgiveness.

Have mercy upon us and forgive us, O Lord.

If we have made no ventures in fellowship, if we have kept in our heart a grievance against another, if we have not sought reconciliation, if we have been eager for the punishment of wrongdoers and slow to seek their redemption,

Have mercy upon us and forgive us, O Lord.

Then, the people still kneeling or bowed, the minister shall rise and say,

Let each of us in silence make confession to God.

After a period of silent prayer the minister and people shall say,

Have mercy upon me, O God, according to thy loving kindness; according to the multitude of thy tender mercies blot out my transgressions. Wash me thoroughly from mine iniquity, and cleanse me from my sin. Create in me a clean heart, O God; and renew a right spirit within me. Amen.

Then the minister shall say,

This is the message we have heard from him, and proclaim to you, that God is light, and in him is no darkness at all. If we walk in the light, as he is in the light, we have fellowship one with another, and the blood of Jesus Christ his Son cleanses us from all sin. If we say we have no sin, we deceive ourselves, and the truth is not in us. If we confess our sins, he is faithful and just, and will forgive our sins, and cleanse us from all unrighteousness.

Here shall be sung a hymn.

THE COVENANT

Then, the people standing, the minister shall say,

And now, beloved, let us bind ourselves with willing bonds to our covenant God, and take the yoke of Christ upon us.

This taking of his yoke upon us means that we are heartily content that he appoint us our place and work, and that he alone be our reward.

Christ has many services to be done; some are easy, others are difficult; some bring honor, others bring reproach; some are suitable to our natural inclinations, and temporal interests, others are contrary to both. In some we may please Christ and please ourselves; in others we cannot please Christ except by denying ourselves. Yet the power to do all these things is assuredly given us in Christ, who strengthens us.

Therefore let us make the covenant of God our own. Let us engage our heart to the Lord, and resolve in his strength never to go back.

Being thus prepared, let us now, in sincere dependence on his grace and trusting in his promises, yield ourselves anew to him.

Here let the people kneel or bow, and the minister say in the name of all,

O Lord God, holy Father, who hast called us through Christ to be partakers in this gracious covenant: We take upon ourselves with joy the yoke of obedience, and engage ourselves, for love of thee, to seek and do thy perfect will. We are no longer our own, but thine.

Then all shall say,

I am no longer my own, but thine. Put me to what thou wilt, rank me with whom thou wilt; put me to doing, put me to suffering; let me be employed for thee or laid aside for thee, exalted for thee or brought low for thee; let me be full, let me be empty; let me have all things, let me have nothing; I freely and heartily yield all things to thy pleasure and disposal.

And now, O glorious and blessed God, Father, Son, and Holy Spirit, thou art mine, and I am thine. So be it. And the covenant which I have made on earth, let it be ratified in heaven. Amen.

Here all shall stand and say or sing responsively,

Lift up your hearts.

We lift them up unto the Lord.

Let us give thanks unto the Lord.

It is meet and right so to do.

It is very meet, right, and our bounden duty that we should at all times and in all places give thanks unto thee, O Lord, holy Father, almighty, everlasting God.

Therefore with angels and archangels, and with all the company of heaven, we laud and magnify thy glorious name, evermore praising thee, and saying:

Holy, holy, holy, Lord God of hosts: Heaven and earth are full of thy glory! Glory be to thee, O Lord most high! Amen.

Then may follow the Holy Communion, beginning with the prayer of consecration; or else immediately a hymn may be sung and a blessing given.

A Service for Epiphany
(TWELFTHNIGHT)

GREETING

The grace of the Lord Jesus Christ be with you.

And also with you.

The splendor of Christ shines upon us.

Praise the Lord!

HYMN: "As with Gladness Men of Old"

PRAYER

The Lord be with you.

And also with you.

Let us pray: *A brief silence.*
God of all glory, by the guidance of a star you led the Wise Men to worship the Christ Child. By the light of faith lead us to your glory in heaven. We ask this through Christ our Lord.

Amen.

ACT OF PRAISE

Here may be sung the Gloria in Excelsis, *or the* Te Deum, *or another canticle of praise.*

FIRST LESSON: Isaiah 60:1-6

PSALM: Psalm 72:1-14

SECOND LESSON: Ephesians 3:1-12

ALLELUIA, HYMN, or ANTHEM

GOSPEL: Matthew 2:1-12

PRAYERS FOR OTHERS

Let us pray for the church and for the world.
Grant, Almighty God, that all who confess your name may be united in your truth, live together in your love, and reveal your glory in the world.
Silence.
Lord, in your mercy,

Hear our prayer.

Guide the people of this land, and of all the nations, in the ways of justice and peace; that we may honor one another and serve the common good.
Silence.
Lord, in your mercy,

Hear our prayer.

Give us all a reverence for the earth as your own creation, that we may use its resources rightly in the service of others and to your honor and glory.
Silence.
Lord, in your mercy,

Hear our prayer.

Comfort and heal all those who suffer in body, mind, or spirit; give them courage and hope in their troubles, and bring them the joy of your salvation.
Silence.
Lord, in your mercy,

Hear our prayer, through Jesus Christ our Lord. Amen.

INVITATION TO THE TABLE AND PEACE

Christ invites to this table all who confess faith in his promises and who intend to live as reconciled people. Let us, as God's forgiven and accepted people, exchange signs of peace and reconciliation with one another. The peace of our Lord Christ be with you all.

And also with you.

Exchange signs of peace.

OFFERING

GREAT THANKSGIVING

The Lord be with you.

And also with you.

Lift up your hearts.

We lift them to the Lord.

Let us give thanks to the Lord our God.

It is right to give our thanks and praise.

It is right, and a good and joyful thing,
always and everywhere to give thanks to you,
Father Almighty, Creator of heaven and earth.

Before the mountains were brought forth
or you had formed the earth,
from everlasting to everlasting you alone are God.
You created light out of darkness
and brought forth life on the earth.
You formed us in your image
and breathed into us the breath of life.
When we turned away, and our love failed,
your love remained steadfast.
You delivered us from captivity,
made covenant to be our sovereign God,
and spoke to us through your prophets.
And so, with your people on earth
and all the company of heaven,
we praise your name and join their unending hymn:

**Holy, holy, holy Lord, God of power and might,
heaven and earth are full of your glory.
Hosanna in the highest.**

**Blessed is he who comes in the name of the Lord.
Hosanna in the highest.**

Holy are you, and blessed is your Son Jesus Christ,
in whom you have revealed yourself,
our light and our salvation.
You sent a star to guide the Magi
to where the Christ was born;
and your signs and witnesses
in every age and through all the world
have led your people from far places to his light.
In his baptism and in his table fellowship
he took his place with sinners.
Your Spirit anointed him to preach good news to the poor,
to proclaim release to the captives
and recovering of sight to the blind,
to set at liberty those who were oppressed,
and to announce that the time had come
when you would save your people.
By the baptism of his suffering, death, and resurrection
you gave birth to your church,
delivered us from slavery to sin and death,
and made with us a new covenant by water and the Spirit.

On the night in which he gave himself up for us
he took bread, gave thanks to you, broke the bread,
gave it to his disciples, and said:
"Take, eat; this is my body which is given for you.
Do this in remembrance of me."

When the supper was over he took the cup,
gave thanks to you, gave it to his disciples, and said:
"Drink from this, all of you;
this is my blood of the new covenant,
poured out for you and for many
for the forgiveness of sins.
Do this, as often as you drink it, in remembrance of me."

And so,
in remembrance of these your mighty acts in Jesus Christ,
we offer ourselves in praise and thanksgiving
as a holy and living sacrifice,

in union with Christ's offering for us,
as we proclaim the mystery of faith.

Christ has died, Christ is risen, Christ will come again.

Pour out your Holy Spirit on us, gathered here,
and on these gifts of bread and wine.
Make them be for us the body and blood of Christ,
that we may be for the world the body of Christ,
redeemed by his blood.

By your Spirit make us one with Christ,
one with each other,
and one in ministry to all the world,
until Christ comes in final victory
and we feast at his heavenly banquet.
Through your Son Jesus Christ,
with the Holy Spirit in your holy church,
and honor and glory is yours, Almighty Father,
now and for ever.

Amen.

THE LORD'S PRAYER

BREAKING THE BREAD

And he was known to them in the breaking of the bread.

PRESENTING THE CUP

The gifts of God for the people of God.

*Here may be sung the traditional "Lamb of God," or a psalm antiphon and verse such as
"O taste and see the goodness of the Lord," Psalm 34, while the ministers and people
begin the communion sharing.*

COMMUNION

*Hymns or psalms during communion: "Go, Tell It on the Mountain," "Heralds of
Christ," "Christ Is the World's True Light," or "Rise, Shine, You People," Psalm
89:1-7; Psalm 72 if not used before, perhaps ending with a meditative choral piece,
followed by silence.*

PRAYER AFTER COMMUNION

The Lord be with you.

And also with you.

Let us pray:
Pour out upon us
the spirit of your love, O Lord,
and unite the wills
of those whom you have fed
with one heavenly food;
through Jesus Christ our Lord.
or
You have given yourself to us, Lord.

Now we give ourselves for others.

Your love has made us a new people;

As a people of love we will serve you with joy.

Your glory has filled our hearts.

Help us to glorify you in all things. Amen.

HYMN: "Christ Is the World's True Light"
        "Go, Tell It on the Mountain"
        "Rise, Shine, You People"

DISMISSAL WITH BLESSING

Now may our Lord Jesus Christ himself,
and God our Father,
who loved us
and gave us eternal comfort and good hope through grace,
comfort your hearts and establish them
in every good work and word.

Amen.

Go in peace to love and serve the Lord.

Amen. Thanks be to God!

POSTLUDE OR FESTIVE MUSIC

A Service for
a Church Anniversary or Homecoming

CALL TO WORSHIP

Behold, how good and pleasant it is when brothers dwell in unity.

Wherefore let us rejoice and offer unto God our praises.

HYMN: "O How Glorious, Full of Wonder"

INVOCATION

O God, who by your Word marvelously works out our reconciliation: Grant, we beseech you, that following the example of our blessed Lord, and walking in the way of your choosing, we may be subjected to you with all our hearts, and united to each other in holy love; through Jesus Christ our Lord. Amen.

CALL TO CONFESSION

Dearly beloved, the Scriptures move us to acknowledge and confess our sins before Almighty God.

PRAYER OF CONFESSION

Almighty and most merciful Father, we have erred and strayed from your ways like lost sheep. We have followed too much the devices and desires of our own hearts. We have offended against your holy laws. We have left undone those things which we ought to have done; and we have done those things which we ought not to have done; and there is no health in us. But you, O Lord, have mercy upon us, miserable offenders. Spare those, O God, who confess their faults. Restore those who are penitent; according to your promises declared unto us in Christ Jesus our Lord. And grant, O most merciful Father for his sake, that we may hereafter live a godly, righteous, and sober life, to the glory of your holy name. Amen.

WORDS OF ASSURANCE

The past is finished and gone, everything has become fresh and new.

THE LORD'S PRAYER

SCRIPTURE LESSON: Ephesians 4

AFFIRMATION OF FAITH

All recite the Apostle's Creed.

GLORIA PATRI

LITANY

Save us, O God, from living in the past and from resting on the work of those who have gone before us. Let us find a new beginning and a new vision, that we may know our task in this place and in this world today.

O God, give us vision.

Enable us to accept the responsibility of our freedom, the burden of our privilege, and so conduct ourselves as to set an example for those who will follow after.

O God, give us courage.

Spare us from the pride that separates and excludes. Defend us from the ignorance that perpetuates injustice and from the indifference that causes hearts to break.

O God, give us understanding.

Being united in this church, sharing in the great mission that you have set before us, let us find in your church a prod to our imagination, a shock to our laziness, and a source of power in doing your will.

O God, give us strength.

O God, who has given us minds to know you and hearts to love you: send your spirit upon us, make us one, and free us to serve you.

Amen.

HYMN: "God of Love and God of Power"

SERMON

OFFERTORY

PRAYER OF DEDICATION

Almighty God, who has led us, through many diverging paths, to this hour in the life of your church, bless we pray you, our church and all us who are a part of its fellowship. Even as we have been united in the body of the church, grant that we may now be united in mind and spirit, that this union may become real in each of our lives.

Pour forth your spirit afresh upon your church. Give us the patience of those who understand and the concern of those who love, that the might of your gentleness may work through us, the mercy of your wrath may speak through us, and that our faith in your unchanging purposes may be continually renewed.

Hear us as we now, in this solemn hour, dedicate ourselves anew to your church and to you, to the end that our church, *(name)*, may, through our service and love, be a more worthy instrument in the realization of your kingdom. Amen.

CHURCH REMINISCENCE

HYMN: "O God, Our Help in Ages Past"

BENEDICTION

"In the Darkness . . . Light"
(A GOOD FRIDAY CANDLELIGHTING SERVICE)

A candlelight service for Good Friday? True, this is a day of darkness, and we shall experience that progressive darkness as we follow Christ on "The Way of the Cross." But from that Cross our Lord spoke seven times—light in the midst of darkness—and we shall celebrate that light with the lighting of our own candles. Already the "Christ Candle" is aglow in the chancel. Toward the end of the service it will be removed for a moment, symbolizing our Lord's death. In that darkness, the sound of the "strepitus" is heard, a harsh noise denoting the closing of the tomb. But then the candle returns, in anticipation of the Resurrection, our Lord's and our own, and we depart in silence to be "the light of the world" ourselves, disciples commissioned to let our lights shine.

THE LIGHTING OF THE SIX CANDLES: Genesis 1:1-4

HYMN: "Thou, Whose Almighty Word"

SCRIPTURE: Psalm 27

The Lord is my Light and my Salvation; whom shall I fear?

The Lord is the stronghold of my life; of whom shall I be afraid?

When evildoers assail me, uttering slanders against me, my adversaries and foes, they shall stumble and fall.

Though a host encamp against me, my heart shall not fear; though war arise against me, yet I will be confident.

One thing have I asked of the Lord, that will I seek after:

That I may dwell in the house of the Lord all the days of my life, to behold the beauty of the Lord, and to inquire in his temple.

For he will hide me in his shelter in the day of trouble:

He will conceal me under the cover of his tent. He will set me high upon a rock.

And now my head shall be lifted up above my enemies round about me;

and I will offer in his tent sacrifices with shouts of joy; I will sing and make melody to the Lord.

Hear, O Lord, when I cry aloud,

Be gracious to me and answer me!

Thou hast said, "Seek ye my face."

My heart says to thee, "Thy face, Lord, do I seek." Hide not thy face from me.

Turn not thy servant away in anger, thou who hast been my help.

Cast me not off, forsake me not, O God of my salvation!

For my father and my mother have forsaken me,

but the Lord will take me up.

Teach me thy way, O Lord; and lead me on a level path because of my enemies.

Give me not up to the will of my adversaries; for false witnesses have risen against me, and they breathe out violence.

I believe that I shall see the goodness of the Lord in the land of the living!

Wait for the Lord; be strong, and let your heart take courage; yea, wait for the Lord!

PRAYER: Isaiah 2:2-5

INTO THE DARKNESS: The Way of the Cross

Reader 1:   John 19:5-16 (Jesus is condemned to death.)
Reader 2:   Mark 15:20-21 (Jesus is led to Calvary.)
Reader 3:   Luke 23:22-32 (Jesus speaks to the women.)
Reader 4:   John 19:23-25*a* (Jesus is stripped of his garments.)
Reader 5:   Mark 15:23-27 (Jesus is nailed to the cross.)
Reader 6:   Matthew 27:39-44 (Jesus is mocked in his agony.)
Reader 7:   Luke 23:44 (Darkness.)

IN THE DARKNESS, LIGHT!

As the individual candles are lit, you are cautioned not to tip a lighted candle! Hold burning candles upright. Tip only unlit candles to receive the flame from your neighbor.

SCRIPTURE: Portions of John 1:1-16

THE SEVEN WORDS FROM THE CROSS
Sung by the congregation or read responsively.

1. Our Savior speaks in grace
   With words of mercy true:
   "Forgive them, Father," thus He prays;
   "They know not what they do."

2. His wondrous pity see!
   Unto the thief He cries:
   "Today, I tell you, you will be
   With Me in Paradise."

3. To Mary, looking on,
   "Behold your son," He says.
   "Behold your mother"; thus on John
   Love's burden gently lays.

4. Now hear the awful cry,
   Sin's dreadful burden see:
   "My God, My God," the Son shouts,
   "Why Have You forsaken Me?"

5. As Man for me He dies.
   Sin's pow'r has done it's worst.
   From hell's dread agony He cries
   A simple word: **"I thirst."**

6. **" 'Tis finished,"** says the Lord.
   The burden on Him laid
   Of sinful thought and deed and word—
   The debt is fully paid.

7. **"Father, into Your hands**
   My spirit I commend."
   And He who hears and understands
   Receives Him in the end.

SCRIPTURE: 2 Corinthians 4:6; I John 1:7

> 8. Beneath the Cross may I
> For whom all this was done
> Repentant and believing cry,
> **"This truly is God's Son!"**

After the candles are extinguished, please stand for prayer, concluding with the Lord's Prayer in unison.

READER 8: Matthew 27:57-60 (Jesus is laid in the tomb.)

"You are the light of the world. A city set on a hill cannot be hid. Nor do men light a lamp and put it under a bushel, but on a stand, and it gives light to all the house. Let your light so shine before men, that they may see your good works and give glory to your Father who is in heaven" (Matthew 5:14-16).

Leave the church in reverent silence . . . and let your light shine!

A Service of Worship for All Saints

GATHERING

GREETING

Grace to you and peace from God
who is, and was, and is to come.

Amen.

And from Jesus Christ the faithful witness,
the first born of the dead,
the ruler of kings on earth.

Amen.

The grace of the Lord Jesus be with all the saints.

Amen.

HYMN OF PRAISE: "For All the Saints"

OPENING PRAYER

God of all holiness,
you gave our saints different gifts on earth

but one holy city in heaven.
Give us grace to follow their good example,
that we may know the joy you have prepared
for all who love you;
through your Son Jesus Christ our Lord.

Amen.

FIRST LESSON

Revelation 7:9-17	(Year A)
Revelation 21:1-6a	(Year B)
Daniel 7:1-3, 15-18	(Year C)

PSALM

Psalm 34:1-10	(Year A)
Psalm 24:1-6	(Year B)
Psalm 149	(Year C)

SECOND LESSON

I John 3:1-3	(Year A)
Colossians 1:9-14	(Year B)
Ephesians 1:11-23	(Year C)

HYMN: "Blest Are the Pure in Heart"

GOSPEL

Matthew 5:1-12	(Year A)
John 11:32-44	(Year B)
Luke 6:20-36	(Year C)

SERMON

[NAMING OF THE HONORED DEAD]

The names of members of the congregation who have died within the past year may be solemnly read, the people standing. A minute of silence follows.

PRAYERS OF THE PEOPLE OR PASTORAL PRAYER

This may begin with a brief silence or with the following:

The Lord be with you.

And also with you.

Let us pray:
Holy God, we pray for your human family everywhere;

That we may be one.

Grant that all who are baptized into Christ may faithfully serve you;

That your name may be glorified on earth as in heaven.

We pray for all bishops, pastors, and deacons;

That there may be justice and peace on the earth.

Give us grace to do your will in all that we undertake;

That our works may find favor in your sight.

Have compassion on those who suffer from any grief or trouble;

That they may be delivered from their distress.

Give to the departed eternal rest;

Let light perpetual shine upon them.

We praise you for your saints who have entered into joy;

May we also come to share in your heavenly kingdom.

Let us pray for our own needs and those of others.
Silence.
The people may add their petitions, following which the presiding minister may add a suitable collect or other brief concluding prayer.

OFFERING

If Holy Communion is not celebrated, the service concludes with a prayer of thanksgiving, the Lord's Prayer, and a dismissal with blessing.

DISMISSAL WITH BLESSING

Go forth into the world in the strength of God's mercy
to live and to serve in newness of life.
May Jesus Christ, the bread of heaven, bless and keep you.

Amen.

May the Lamb of God who laid down his life for all,
  graciously smile upon you.

Amen.

May the Lord God order all your days and deeds in peace.

Amen. Thanks be to God.

"We Thank Thee, O God"
(A SERVICE OF THANKSGIVING)

Shirley N. Morgan, Jr.

PRELUDE

OPENING HYMN: "Rejoice, Ye Pure in Heart"

CALL TO WORSHIP

O give thanks unto the Lord. Call upon his name; make known his deeds among the people.

Sing unto him, sing psalms unto him; talk ye of all his wondrous words.

Glory ye in his holy name; let the heart of them rejoice that seek the Lord.

Amen.

INVOCATION

With deep gratitude and joy, O our God, we come into thy courts to offer prayers of praise and thanksgiving. All that we are, we owe to thee; all that we have is a gift from thy hand. Earth and sky, rain and sunshine, flower and fruit, all the beauty and bounty of nature, attune our souls to thoughts of thy beneficence. Grant, O God, that this festival may bring gladness to our homes. May we share our blessings with the needy and lift the burden of care from the heavy-laden, that all may celebrate this day in joy before thee. Amen.

HYMN OF AFFIRMATION: "We Plow the Fields"

SCRIPTURE: Psalm 105:1-5, 106:1-2

SILENT PRAYER

PASTORAL PRAYER

ANTHEM

MINISTER'S MESSAGE

OFFERING

DOXOLOGY

LITANY OF THANKSGIVING:

For the abundance of your gifts to us in the days that are past, and for the promise of steadfast grace in the days that are ahead,

We give thee thanks, O Lord.

For life and health; for the strength of mind and heart; for the common things which come with every day and hour,

We bless thy name, O Lord.

For home, for family, for friends, for all those blessings by which life becomes more meaningful and time more precious; and for the love which is ours in Christ Jesus our Lord,

We give thee thanks, O God.

In grateful acknowledgment that these gifts of life are ours through your merciful grace,

We give ourselves to you, O God, and praise thy name forever.

HYMN OF THANKSGIVING: "Now Thank We All Our God"

BENEDICTION

"The Hanging of the Greens"

(A SERVICE FOR THE FIRST SUNDAY OF ADVENT)

Sally Rhodes Ahner

PRELUDE

PROCESSIONAL HYMN: "Come, Thou Long-Expected Jesus"

During the singing of the hymn, the greens may be brought in and one Advent candle lit.

LITANY OF THE GREENS

How shall we prepare this house for the coming of Jesus, the King?

With branches of cedar, the tree of royalty.

How shall we prepare this house for the coming of Jesus, the eternal Christ?

With garlands of pine and fir, whose leaves are ever living, ever green.

How shall we prepare this house for the coming of Jesus, our Savior?

With wreaths of holly and ivy, symbolizing his passion, death, and resurrection.

How shall we prepare our hearts for the coming of Jesus, the son of God?

By hearing again the words of the prophets who foretold the saving work of God.

For God did not send the Son into the world to condemn the world, but that the world through him might be saved.

Glory to God in the highest!

FIRST READING

Reader 1: The prophet proclaims good news to a people in exile.

SCRIPTURE: Isaiah 40:1-5

HYMN: "O Come, O Come, Emmanuel"

SECOND READING

Reader 1: The Lord promises to send the people a righteous king.

SCRIPTURE: Jeremiah 23:5-6

Reader 2: In ancient times the cedar was revered as the tree of royalty. It also signified immortality, and was used for purification. We place this cedar branch in the sanctuary as a symbol of Christ, who reigns as king forever, and whose coming, in justice and righteousness, will purify our hearts.

HYMN: "Joy to the World" (first verse)

THIRD READING

Reader 1: The prophet announces the reign of the Messiah.

SCRIPTURE: Isaiah 9:2, 6-7

Reader 2: Because the needles of the pine and fir trees do not die each season like the leaves of most trees, the ancients saw them as symbols of things that last forever. In the scripture passage just read, the prophet Isaiah tells us that there will be no end to the reign of the Messiah, and so we hang this wreath of evergreens shaped in a circle, which itself has no end, to signify the eternal kingdom of Jesus, the Christ.

HYMN: "Joy to the World" (last verse)

FOURTH READING

Reader 1: The prophet tells of the healing power of the Anointed One.

SCRIPTURE: Isaiah 61:1-3

Reader 2: Because this is the passage which Jesus reads at the beginning of his ministry in the synagogue at Nazareth, and which he applied to himself, we cannot hear these words of Isaiah without thinking of the healing that the coming of the Christ will bring. The evergreen most associated with healing properties in the ancient world was the mistletoe. It was called the "all-healer." People thought its special powers came from the lightning bolt that fixed it high up in a tree, and therefore, they believed it came, as did the lightning, from heaven itself. This healing power was not only for physical ailments, but for the healing of relationships as well. It is said that in one town in medieval England, a bough of mistletoe was brought in and put on the altar, and the priest then declared a pardon for all sins. Originally, the kiss under the mistletoe was thought to have been the "kiss of peace," symbolizing reconciliation, not the romantic kiss of boy and girl. It is in keeping with this more ancient meaning that we decorate this house with mistletoe, in anticipation of the coming of the healing presence of Jesus the Christ.

HYMN: "Joy to the World" (third verse)

FIFTH READING

Reader 1: The prophet describes the redeemer of Israel as the Suffering Servant.

SCRIPTURE: Isaiah 53:1-6

Reader 2: Tradition holds that this passage from Isaiah describes the sufferings of Jesus, who saved us from our sins by his death on the cross, and by his being raised from the dead. In ancient times, the holly was considered the symbol of Christ's passion: its prickly leaves suggested the crown of thorns, its red berries the blood of the Savior, and its bitter bark the drink offered to Jesus on the cross. As we hang the holly, let us rejoice in the coming of Jesus, our Savior.

CAROL: "The Holly and the Ivy"

All:　　　The holly and the ivy,
　　　　　When they are both full grown,
　　　　　Of all the trees that are in the wood,
　　　　　The holly bears the crown.

All:　　　*Refrain:*
　　　　　O the rising of the sun,
　　　　　And the running of the deer,
　　　　　The playing of the merry organ,
　　　　　Sweet singing in the choir.

Women:　　The holly bears a blossom,
　　　　　As white as the lily flower,
　　　　　And Mary bore sweet Jesus Christ
　　　　　To be our sweet Savior.

All:　　　*Refrain*

Men:　　　The holly bears a berry,
　　　　　As red as any blood,
　　　　　And Mary bore sweet Jesus Christ
　　　　　To do poor sinners good.

All:　　　*Refrain*

Choir or　The holly bears a prickle,
Solo:　　　As sharp as any thorn,
　　　　　And Mary bore sweet Jesus Christ
　　　　　On Christmas Day in the morn.

All: *Refrain*

All: The holly bears a bark,
                As bitter as any gall,
                And Mary bore sweet Jesus Christ
                For to redeem us all.

All: *Refrain*

SIXTH READING

Reader 1: Let us stand to hear the words of the Evangelist as he tells of the coming of the Light of the World.

SCRIPTURE: John 1:1-5, 9-14

Reader 2: As our final preparation for the coming of Jesus, the Light of the World, we will light the Christmas tree. And in this time of Advent, whenever you see a lighted Christmas tree, let it call to mind the One who brings light to our darkness, healing to our unwholeness, and peace to all who will receive him.

CAROL: "O Christmas Tree"

BENEDICTION

POSTLUDE

"A Christmas Candlelighting Service"

Shirley N. Morgan, Jr.

PRELUDE

OPENING HYMN: "O Come, All Ye Faithful"

CALL TO WORSHIP

Behold, I bring you good news of great joy which will come to all people;

For to you is born this day in the city of David, a Savior, who is Christ the Lord.

Come let us worship the Lord who established a new covenant through his son Jesus Christ.

We come in spirit and in truth.

THE ANGEL GABRIEL VISITS MARY

SCRIPTURE: Luke 1:26-33

HYMN: "Come, Thou Long-Expected Jesus"

MARY AND JOSEPH GO TO BETHLEHEM

SCRIPTURE: Luke 2:1-5

HYMN: "O Little Town of Bethlehem"

THE BIRTH IN THE MANGER

SCRIPTURE: Luke 2:6-7

HYMN: "There's a Song in the Air"

THE ANGELS' SONG

SCRIPTURE: Luke 2:8-14

HYMN: "Angels, from the Realms of Glory"

THE SHEPHERDS' RESPONSE

SCRIPTURE: Luke 2:15-20

HYMN: "Good Christian Men, Rejoice"

LIGHTING OF THE CHRIST CANDLE

The white color signifies the pure life of Christ; the flame is a symbol of Christ, the Light of the World.

PRAYER OF ILLUMINATION

In unison:
Almighty and everlasting God, who brought the Gentiles to thy light, and made known to them him who is the true light and the bright and morning star: fill us, we beseech thee, with thy glory and bring the radiance of thy light unto all nations, through Jesus Christ our Lord. Amen.

HYMN: "Hark! the Herald Angels Sing"

SILENT PRAYER

PASTORAL PRAYER

ANTHEM

MINISTER'S MESSAGE

OFFERING

SERVICE OF CANDLELIGHTING

As "Silent Night" is being sung, the lights will be dimmed, and the minister will light a candle from the Christ Candle. The minister will then light the candles of the first worshiper in each pew. Light will then be passed from worshiper to worshiper. Remember that the lighted candle remains upright, and the unlighted candle is tipped to the lighted. Before leaving the pew, worshipers are requested to extinguish their candles.

HYMN: "Silent Night"

PRAYER OF SUPPLICATION

In unison:
In this season of lights, enlighten our lives. Every time we see a star in the sky, cause us to rejoice in your coming to break the monotony of our darkness. Every time we see colored Christmas lights on a tree, remind us of the glory of your coming. Every time we see a candle lighted in this season, bring to our remembrance how you are the Light of the World. Amen.

HYMN OF AFFIRMATION: "Joy to the World"

BENEDICTION

A Service for Rally Day

PRELUDE

CALL TO WORSHIP
O God, open our lips.

And our mouths shall show forth your praise.

Praise the Lord.

HYMN OF PRAISE

PRAYER OF INVOCATION

In unison:
O God, grant that we may love you with all our heart, with all our mind, and with all our strength. Grant that we may love our neighbors according to your grace and live at peace with all people. Cleanse our hearts of envy, impatience, and ill will. Fill us with kindness and compassion that we may rejoice in the happiness and success of others and share with them in their sorrows, So we may live and work together as your children in the spirit of Jesus Christ our Lord. Amen.

THE LORD'S PRAYER

SCRIPTURE LESSON: Jonah 3 and 4

PASTORAL PRAYER

PRAYER HYMN: "Dear Lord and Father of Mankind"

OFFERING

DOXOLOGY

SERMON: (Suggested topic, "The Church As a Family")

LITANY OF DEDICATION

To be entered into by all in the mood of prayer.

And God formed man of the dust of the ground, and breathed into his nostrils the breath of life. Likewise God fashioned woman from the rib of the man; and they became living souls.

That you made us for yourself and that our hearts are restless until they rest in you, we thank you, O God.

The God that made the world and all things in it gives to all life and breath; and God made from one all the nations of people to dwell on the face of the earth.

That you have set your divine life in all life, we thank you, O God.

God set the solitary in families, and said to Abraham, In your seed shall all the families of the earth be blessed.

For the rich heritage of parenthood and the Christ-likeness of childhood, we thank you, O God.

Train up children in the way they should go, and even when they are old they will not depart from it. And Jesus set a child in their midst.

For the fresh revelation of yourself in each little child, and for the bonds of love which bind childhood, youth, and maturity together—we thank you, O God.

Jesus looked round about on them that sat about him and said, Behold my mother and my brethren! For whosoever shall do the will of God, the same is my brother, and sister, and mother.

That belonging to one family is so clearly shown in the Scriptures and in the life of your Son—we thank you, O God.

Now are we the children of God, and members one of another.

All: To the divine relationship as children of our Heavenly Father, we dedicate ourselves, our souls and bodies to be living sacrifices unto you, O God. For their sakes—for all your children—we consecrate ourselves gladly to teach and willingly to learn the Way, the Truth, and the Life, that your whole family may be redeemed through Jesus Christ. Amen.

HYMN: "Joyful, Joyful, We Adore Thee"

BENEDICTION

POSTLUDE

A Service for Promotion Day

PRELUDE

PROCESSIONAL: "And Are We Yet Alive"

CALL TO WORSHIP
O come, let us worship and bow down.

Let us kneel before the Lord our Maker!

SONG *(by preschoolers)*: "Jesus Loves Me"

PROMOTION OF PRESCHOOLERS

SONG *(by youth choir)*: "I've Found a Friend"

UNISON READING *(by children from middle school)*: Psalm 100; Matthew 5:1-12

PROMOTION OF YOUNGER AND
MIDDLE ELEMENTARY DEPARTMENTS

During the presentation of certificates and/or Bibles, congregation and choir may sing "Open My Eyes, That I May See."

BIBLE VERSE RECITATIONS *(by older elementary children)*

Some suggestions: Luke 2:52; Genesis 8:22; Psalm 24:1; Matthew 25:40; Psalm 104:33; Matthew 22:37, 39; John 15:14; Isaiah 41:6; Psalm 118:24; Psalm 100:2; Psalm 33:12; Psalm 119:11; Psalm 86:5; Psalm 67:3

PROMOTION OF OLDER ELEMENTARY CHILDREN

During the presentation of certificates the congregation and choir may sing "O Word of God Incarnate."

PASTORAL PRAYER

LORD'S PRAYER

OFFERING: (Offering verse, Luke 6:38)

DOXOLOGY

SCRIPTURE READING *(by a young person)*: Acts 2:1-7, 16-17

HYMN: "Come, Christians, Join to Sing"

BENEDICTION

"The Lord bless you, and keep you: The Lord make his face to shine upon you, and be gracious to you: The Lord lift up his countenance upon you, and give you peace" (Numbers 6:24-26). Amen.

A Blessing of Animals and Pets

SONG: "Shout from the Highest Mountain" *or* "All Things Bright and Beautiful"

INTRODUCTORY REMARKS

SCRIPTURE: Psalm 148

BLESSING OF ANIMALS AND PETS

Let us pray: O God, our heavenly Father, we worship you, we adore you. You have made this world so beautiful. In it you have placed so many species of animals. All of them give you glory. We thank you for all of them, especially for all those present here this morning.

We are so deeply grateful, O God, for all the pleasure and joy these animals, these pets, have brought not only to the children here but also to the adults.

By your word, Almighty God, all things are made holy. We pray that you will pour down your blessings on these animals and pets. Grant that all those present who give thanks to you and who take good care of these animals may receive through your almighty power health of body and protection of soul. We pray that you will keep these pets and animals safe from all harm and take care of them in your divine providence.

We ask these blessings, O God, as we ask for all good things through Jesus Christ, our Lord in the unity of the Holy Spirit. Amen.

CLOSING REMARKS

HYMN: "Now Thank We All Our God"

A Blessing for a Civil Marriage

The persons whose marriage is to be blessed stand before the minister in public worship, the husband on the right hand of his wife.

After a hymn the minister says:

We are gathered here in the presence of God to ask his blessing on *(Name)* and *(Name)*'s marriage. Christian marriage is a gift and calling of God, entered in obedience to the gospel of Christ. Today *(Name)* and *(Name)* give thanks for that gift, and acknowledge that calling.

We declare that

God has provided marriage for the companionship of help and comfort in mutual care, so that husband and wife may live faithfully together.

God has provided it for the fulfilling of human love in mutual honor, so that husband and wife may know each other with delight.

[God has provided it for the birth and nurture of children, so that they may find the security of love, and grow up in the heritage of faith.]

God has provided it for the enrichment of society, so that husband and wife being joined together may enter into the life of the community as a new creation.

PRAYER

God our Father
your generous love surrounds us,
and everything we enjoy comes from you.
We confess our ingratitude for your goodness,
and our selfishness in the use of your gifts.
We ask you to forgive us,
and to fill us with true thankfulness,
through Jesus Christ our Savior. **Amen.**

O God,
you have taught us through Jesus
that love is the fulfilling of the law.
Grant to your servants,
that, loving one another,
they may continue in your love until their lives' end;
through the same Jesus Christ our Lord. **Amen.**

THE PROMISE

All stand and the minister says to the husband:

(Name), have you taken *(Name)* to be your [lawful wedded] wife.
Since you wish to acknowledge before God your desire that your married life should be according to his will,
I ask you, therefore,
will you love her, comfort her, honor and protect her, in times of prosperity and health,
and in times of trouble and suffering,
and be faithful to her as long as you both shall live?

I will.

The minister then says to the wife:

(Name), you have taken (Name) to be your [lawful wedded] husband.
Since you wish to acknowledge before God your desire that your married life
should be according to his will,
I ask you, therefore,
will you love him, comfort him, honor and protect him, in times of prosperity and
health,
and in times of trouble and suffering,
and be faithful to him as long as you both shall live?

I will.

THE BLESSING

The husband and wife kneel and the minister says:

God the Father give you joy.
God the Son give you new life.
God the Holy Spirit unite you.

The Lord bless you and watch over you;
The Lord make his face shine upon you and be gracious to you;
the Lord look kindly on you and give you peace.

May the One God
present with you now
keep you true to each other.

May the ring(s) you wear be the symbol(s) of unending love, and reminder of the
covenant made this day.

May you love and cherish each other till death parts you.

And to God be the praise for ever. **Amen.**

The couple stand, join their right hands, and the minister says:

Those whom God has joined together, man must not separate.

A hymn may be sung.

*The service may continue with prayers for the couple, for Christian family life, for the gift
of children, and for concerns outside the family, and with the Lord's Prayer.*

The service may conclude with the Lord's Supper from the offertory, or with a hymn and a dismissal and blessing.

A Service for Healing

This service is a guide. Every act of public worship and all services arranged by the church will always serve in some way to help people who are ill. This service particularly emphasizes our desire to be made well, and suggests where and how the church might follow Jesus in the "Laying on of Hands."

WELCOME AND NOTICES

The minister shall briefly explain the purpose of the service.

CALL TO WORSHIP

How good it is to give thanks to the Lord, to sing in your honor, Most High God, to proclaim your constant love every morning, and your faithfulness every night. Jesus said: Whoever believes in me will do the works I do—Yes; he will do even greater ones, because I am going to the Father. And I will do whatever you ask in my name.

PRAYER OF APPROACH

Father God, Creator of the universe and fashioner of men and women in your image, we worship and adore you.
Lord Jesus, Savior of the world and friend of each one of us, we worship and adore you.
Holy Spirit, life of the church and comforter of the needy, we worship and adore you.
One God, you are constantly bringing us fellowship and blessing; help us to open our hearts and lives to your coming in this time of worship. **Amen.**

HYMN

PRAYERS OF CONFESSION

We confess to you Lord, what we are:
    we are not the people we like others to think we are;
    we are afraid to admit even to ourselves what lies in the depths of our souls,
    But we do not want to hide our true selves from you.

We believe that you know us as we are, and yet you love us.
Help us to know and accept ourselves; give us the courage to put our trust in your forgiveness, through Christ our Savior. **Amen.**

Silence for a personal confession of sin, or:

Lord God, we confess:
we have forgotten you and failed in our relationships with others;
we have been fearful about ourselves and anxious about the future;
we have spoken hard and bitter words;
we have been boastful of our achievements and envious of the success of others;
we have selfishly pursued our own ends and given little time or thought for the needs of others.
Creator and Father, you have made us to live in harmony and fellowship with you and each other; we have become divided within and separated from the source of our strength and joy through our failure to seek you regularly in prayer.
Lord of our life and our helper at all times, forgive us and enable us to forgive others, in the name of Christ our Savior. **Amen.**

ASSURANCE OF PARDON

Here are words you may trust, words that merit full acceptance:
"Christ Jesus came into the world to save sinners." To all who confess their sins and resolve to lead a new life he says:
"Your sins are forgiven," and he also says:
"Follow me."
Now to the King of all worlds, immortal, invisible, the only wise God, be honor and glory for ever and ever. **Amen.**

PROCLAMATION OF THE WORD OF GOD

Reading of Scripture and any other appropriate reading by which God's goodness, mercy, and caring concern for his people are set forth.

PRAYERS OF THANKSGIVING

Lord God, accept our thanks for everything that speaks to us of your love, enriches our lives, and gives purpose to our days.
We give thanks for the world of nature, providing for our bodily needs; for home and family life in which we share so much happiness and find your love made real; for daily work and tasks to do, and the satisfaction which comes from those well done.

We give thanks for the coming of your Son to live our life and to give us his victory over sin and death. For his teaching, preaching, and healing whereby he declared your Fatherhood, revealing your power to save those who put their trust in you, we give thanks and praise. For his Church in every age we praise your name, thanking you for those who have handed down to us such a rich heritage of Christian witness and service. May we in our day continue steadfast, courageous and true to our ever-living Lord, that men and women everywhere may rejoice to see your power at work in us; through Jesus Christ our Lord. **Amen.**

SERMON

SILENT MEDITATION

During which worshipers are invited to meditate on the readings and the sermon.

HYMN

OFFERING AND DEDICATION

PRAYERS OF INTERCESSION

Lord God, we ask you to hear us as we bring before you in prayer the needs of others.

We pray for the Church, its life and work:
> Lord of the Church, we rejoice in your cross, and ask that your sacrificial love may become the example of all your followers. May your constant presence be our inspiration and power to overcome evil, your gospel become the hope of all peoples.

We pray for the sick, and all in need of healing:
> Father of us all, we rejoice in your creating and providential love, and ask that you will heal the sick, comfort the sorrowing, and reassure the anxious and despairing. Give them peace, and the knowledge that none is outside your love and care. Hear our prayer for our friends who are sick and for all who have requested our prayers, especially those whom we now name. . . .

We pray for those who work for the well-being and healing of others:
> Holy Spirit, we rejoice in your life-giving power, and ask that you will use the skills of doctors, nurses, and all who serve the sick. Give them love and compassion, that they may be your ministers of healing.

Lord God, we bring to you these our prayers, and ask you to use them to further your gracious purpose for your world: in the name of Jesus Christ, the healer of all our sickness. **Amen.**

THE LORD'S PRAYER

THE LAYING ON OF HANDS

Invite those wishing this ministry to come forward.

PRAYER FOR HEALING

Lord Jesus, the same yesterday, today, and for ever, let your healing power be upon those who seek your help at this time. Grant them new life and strength.

Each person should then come forward to kneel if possible.

(Name) may the Lord Christ grant you healing and renewal, according to his will. Go in peace.

The person returns to his place.

PRAYER OF THANKSGIVING

Father, we thank you that you have granted to each of us a spiritual blessing, and that you are granting healing to your servants. Help us, refreshed by your presence, to go into the world, to serve you in the power of the Holy Spirit, through Jesus Christ our Lord. **Amen.**

HYMN

DISMISSAL AND BLESSING

A Service of Thanksgiving for the Birth or Adoption of a Child

This service is intended primarily for use within a corporate service of worship. When conducted apart from the fuller liturgical context, appropriate modifications may be made. One or more of the following Scripture passages may be used in the service of worship:

Deuteronomy 6:4-7
Diligently teach your children.
Deuteronomy 31:12-13
"Do . . . this law . . . that their children . . . may hear and learn."
I Samuel 1:9-11, 20-28; 2:26
The birth and presentation of Samuel
Psalm 8
"O Lord, our Lord, how majestic is thy name in all the earth!"
Psalm 78:1-7
Tell to the coming generations the glorious deeds of the Lord.
Matthew 18:1-4
Those who humble themselves like children will be greatest.
Mark 10:13-16
Jesus blesses the children.
Luke 2:22-32, 52
The presentation of Jesus in the temple.

PRESENTATION

Members of Christ's family, I present to you *(Name)* and *(Name)* together with *(Name)*, whose coming into their home they now acknowledge with gratitude and faith.

CALL TO THANKSGIVING

Within the family of Christ, the birth or adoption of a child is an occasion for thanksgiving. Life is God's gift, and children are a heritage from the Lord. Therefore we who are entrusted with their care are given both great responsibility and opportunity. Because God has favored us through the coming of this child, let us offer our praise.

HYMN OF PRAISE, PSALM, OR CANTICLE

PRAYER

For the birth of a child, the following or another prayer is offered.

O God, like a mother who comforts her children, you strengthen us in our solitude, sustain and provide for us. We come before you with gratitude for the gift of this child, for the joy which has come into this family, and the grace with which you surround them and all of us. As a father cares for his children, so continually look upon us with compassion and goodness. Pour out your Spirit. Enable your servants to abound in love, and establish our homes in holiness; through Jesus Christ our Lord. **Amen.**

For the adoption of a child, the following or another prayer is offered.

O God, you have adopted all of us as your children. We give thanks to you for the child who has come to bless this family and for the parents who have welcomed this child as their own. By the power of your Holy Spirit, fill their home with love, trust, and understanding; through Jesus Christ our Lord. **Amen.**

NAMING OF THE CHILD

Minister: What name have you given this child?
Those presenting the child respond.
However, if the name is to be conferred as part of this order, the minister instead asks:
What name do you now give this child?
Those presenting the child may place their hands upon the child.
They respond:
We name you *(Name).*

THANKSGIVING

Minister to family: In accepting *(Name)* as a gift from God, you also acknowledge your faith in Jesus Christ and the responsibility which God places upon you.

The members of the family respond, saying or repeating after the minister:
We receive *(Name)*
from the hand of a loving Creator.
With humility and hope
we accept the obligation which is ours
to love and nurture *(her/him)*
and to lead *(her/him)* to Christian faith
by our teaching and example.
We ask for the power of the Holy Spirit
and the support of the church
that we may be good stewards
of this gift of life.

Minister to congregation: The church is the family of Christ, the community in which we grow in faith and commitment.

Congregation: **We rejoice to take *(Name)* under our care. We seek God's grace to be a community in which the gospel is truly proclaimed to all. We will support you and minister with you as workers together in Christ Jesus and heirs of his promise.**

The minister takes the child and says:

(Name), may the eternal God bless you and watch over you. May Jesus Christ incorporate you in his death and resurrection through baptism.
(If the child has previously been baptized, delete "through baptism.")
May the Holy Spirit sanctify you and bring you to life everlasting.
The minister returns the child to the family.

PRAYER

Gracious God, from whom every family in heaven and on earth is named: Out of the treasures of your glory strengthen us through your Spirit. Help us joyfully to nurture *(Name)* within your church. Bring *(her/him)* to baptism (or to Christian maturity), that Christ may dwell in *(her/his)* heart through faith. Give power to *(Name)* and to us, that with all your people we may grasp the breadth and length, the height and depth, of Christ's love. Enable us to know this love, though it is beyond knowledge, and to be filled with your own fullness; through Jesus Christ our Lord. Amen.

If the Lord's Prayer is not used at another point in the service, it may be prayed by all here.

ASCRIPTION

Glory to God, who by the power at work among us is able to do far more than we can ask or imagine. Glory be given to this God from generation to generation in the church and in Christ Jesus forever! **Amen.**

A Service for the Consecration of a Dwelling

SCRIPTURE SENTENCE

"Behold, I stand at the door and knock; if any one hears my voice and opens the door, I will come in" (Revelation 3:20).

DECLARATION OF PURPOSE

Dear friends, we have gathered here to seek God's blessing upon this house, which by the favor of God and human labor has been so far completed. A house is not only our dwelling but a symbol to us of God's loving care and of our life together as the family of Christ. Let us therefore bring praise and thanksgiving for goodness and mercy and for our communion, offering ourselves as God's servants and as loving sisters and brothers to one another.

OPENING PRAYER

Let us pray.
Eternal God, you govern all things in heaven and earth, and make all things new through your almighty Word. We thank you for your faithfulness and bless your holy name. Shed your rays of light upon this household that those who live *(the one who lives)* here may be confident of your guidance and walk with steady faith. Be close in time of stress or pain and give courage and hope that never fails; through Jesus Christ our Lord. **Amen.**

SCRIPTURE LESSON: I John 4:11-21 or Ephesians 3:14-21

ACT OF CONSECRATION

In the name of the Father, and of the Son, and of the Holy Spirit, we consecrate this home, committing to God's love and care this house and all who dwell *(the one who dwells)* therein. **Amen.**

CLOSING PRAYER

Let us pray.
Eternal God, bless this home. Let your love rest upon it and your promised presence be manifested in it. May the members of this household *(Name)* grow in grace and in the knowledge of our Lord Jesus Christ. Teach them *(him/her)* to love, as you have given us commandment; and help us all to live in the peace of Jesus Christ our Lord. **Amen.**

The service may conclude here with the Lord's Prayer and blessing.

A Service of Cleansing

(FOOTWASHING)

A service of footwashing usually occurs with some other elements of worship—perhaps before communion. It is often celebrated on Holy Thursday to remind us of Christ's actions in the Upper Room. The congregation should know well in advance so that those who wish to participate can come suitably attired. Depending on the congregation, only certain representatives may participate, or the entire body. Persons should come forward to the basins as they feel led to participate.

PRELUDE: "What Wondrous Love Is This?"

CALL TO WORSHIP: Genesis 2:4-10

HYMN: "Come, Thou Fount of Every Blessing"

SCRIPTURE LESSON: John 13:1-11

Jesus loved them to the end. To show his love, he rose from the table, laid aside his garments, and girded himself with a towel. Then he poured water into a basin and began to wash the disciples' feet. As a response to our hearing the word, let us now commemorate this act in response to his commandment—that we love one another as he has loved us.

The service may continue with the partaking of Holy Communion. The offering should be brought to the altar.

HYMN: "There's a Wideness in God's Mercy"

BENEDICTION

Like Pilate, we can wash our hands of Jesus; like the woman who washed his feet with her tears, we can come to him, humbly seeking forgiveness; like Jesus our Lord, we can learn to show our love by washing one another. As we go now, the decision is up to us—we can wash our hands of him, or for him. **Amen.**